THE GAIN CYCLE

Holistic health is the future of fitness

Tanya "Taz" Dunstan

Copyright © 2025
First Published in Australia in 2025
By Morpheus Publishing
Geelong Victoria 3216
www.morpheuspublishing.com.au

All rights reserved. No part of this publication may be reproduced, stored in a retrieval system, or transmitted in any form or by any means, electronic, mechanical, photocopying, recording or otherwise, without the prior written permission of the publisher or author.

Paperback ISBN:	978-1-7642622-3-1
Author:	Tania (Taz) Dunstan
Editor:	Justine Martin
Cover Graphics:	Mylan Carascal

A catalogue record for this book is available from the National Library of Australia.

DISCLAIMER
The information contained in this book is for general informational purposes only. The author and publisher are not offering any medical, legal or professional advice. While every effort has been made to ensure the accuracy and completeness of the information provided, the author and publisher assume no responsibility for errors or omissions or any outcomes or consequences resulting from using this book's content.

PHOTOGRAPHS
All photographs used in this publication are credited to Darren Burns and Shaun Poh. They are used with permission. Unauthorised reproduction or use of these images is strictly prohibited.

COPYRIGHT
All original material in this book is the sole property of the author and Morpheus Publishing.

DISTRIBUTION
This book is distributed by Morpheus Publishing and is available through authorised distributors, booksellers, Morpheus Publishing website.

COPYRIGHT PERMISSIONS
For copyright permissions or any other inquiries, please contact:

PUBLISHER: Morpheus Publishing
www.morpheuspublishing.com.au || hello@justinemartin.com.au || +61403 564 942

AUTHOR: Tania (Taz) Dunstan
www.morpheuspublishing.com.au/authors/tanya-(taz)-dunstan

TABLE OF CONTENTS

1: The Gain Cycle 1

2: Who is the Gain Cycle for? 5

3: Will it work? 7

4: What do I need? 9

5: Where do I start? 19

6: About the Author 41

Testimonials 45

Tanya (Taz) Dunstan Contact Details 51

THE GAIN CYCLE

THE GAIN CYCLE

A world first designed to help people survive and then thrive - from where you are, to where you want to be in small, easily achievable steps.

The Gain Cycle is the world's answer to the "Pain Cycle" of equal and opposite effect. Designed by Tanya Taz Dunstan, a health and fitness professional of over 19 years of industry experience, to establish a sustainable lifestyle focused on optimal health and genuine happiness in 21 days.

This program does not involve strict meal plans and extensive exercise regimes. It is not expensive, time-consuming, exhausting, difficult or impractical. What it does is encompass a lot of elements you would encounter on most days, usually without giving them much attention. The program challenges you to become more self-aware of your triggers and behaviours, which enables you to rationally respond to situations and stressors instead of just reacting to them, or feeling victimised by them, resorting to old, potentially unhealthy habits. The gain cycle breaks and replaces the pain cycle!

What was the motivation behind the Gain Cycle?

I have motivated myself previously with short-term goals such as the "Reset" program, designed to focus on self-care and intensive training for a 10-day body transformation to get "comp fit". This worked as a short term goal, like most "diets" but it did not address my stressors or emotional wellbeing. It served as a distraction to get me to an end result, after which point I again returned to a state of sadness. Classic "yo-yo" scenario.

After suffering extreme depression, shock, grief, emotional devastation, severe stress and anxiety, this has taken a psychological, emotional and physical toll on me. I have felt sick, sad and without purpose or motivation regularly. I have been so stressed that I have been shaking with excessive adrenaline and cortisol in my body. I have not been able to switch my brain off, which has kept me up at all hours of the night and then made me feel groggy and fatigued the next day. I have been fueled by caffeine and stress. This is a toxic cycle that I needed to break consciously- to rebuild and heal.

Everything in the body is interconnected, and as such, my emotional state affected me physiologically. I have been losing my hair due to stress. I have lost weight, mostly due to muscle loss and am unable to stomach the idea of food, which made food replacements and liquids essential to rebuild my appetite, working up to solids. This made me feel weak and self-conscious, so I started "calorie loading" eating large amounts of refined breads and chocolate to maintain weight, to avoid "looking sick". My body responded, like most, by depositing massive stores of cellulite around my legs and glutes. I generally felt like my body wasn't mine anymore.

To change this situation, I set very low and achievable goals (out of fear of failure and lack of motivation as much as anything), such as "If I have a shower at any time today that will be a win."

I didn't always reach that goal, but I tried, and that's what counts. As long as you achieve more times than you fail - you will keep progressing. It is hard to empathise, let alone understand what "depression" or "rock bottom" feels like until you have experienced a pain or trauma so significant you literally feel like a dead man (or woman) walking. For that ability to relate, I am grateful to have made it to the other side to speak to those who can't see a way out. This was literally designed for you by someone who has been where you are and knew they couldn't keep going like that.

Everyone's journey is different, and everyone's experiences are unique to them. Whatever low you are experiencing, that state of "survival" you engage in will not lift you out of the depths of despair. It is essential to be aware of that fact in order to make conscious decisions to change. I had my blood pressure and blood tests taken in mid July 2019, and for the first time in my life, I had high blood pressure and my bloods showed elevated levels of cortisol, cholesterol and a low white blood cell count. Not life-threatening for a short time period, but a wake-up call to shock me into action. The Gain Cycle was designed out of necessity as a lifeline for me to reclaim my happiness and prioritise my health. That is what I want to share with others to offer an easy-to-follow, customisable template for anyone at any stage of life, to design a lifestyle that makes them happier, healthier, more driven, and able, to achieve their goals and improve their quality of life.

NOTES

_____

_____

_____

_____

_____

_____

_____

THE GAIN CYCLE

NOTES

WHO IS THE GAIN CYCLE FOR?

Everyone! The Gain Cycle is an all-inclusive program with a focus on improved health and wellbeing designed to help people of all ages, sexes, ethnicities, backgrounds, religious beliefs, lifestyles, fitness levels, health conditions, dietary requirements from those at "ground zero" - the lowest of lows devoid of any direction of drive, right up to busy executives who require more balance and better time management to ensure their health and vitality, and everyone in between.

Quality of life cannot be bought, nor can your health or happiness. People deserve to have access to resources that will encourage positivity, holistic health and genuine wellbeing. This emotional and psychological wellbeing, coupled with some nutritional and exercise knowledge, guarantees an effective and efficient mind, body and soul program.

NOTES

_____

_____

_____

_____

NOTES

WILL IT WORK?

The Gain Cycle is based on undeniable facts of life and supported by science. If you eat well (*nutrient-rich, balanced meals), keep hydrated, exercise regularly and remain consistent with this routine, your body will respond positively.

Most exercise programs and meal plans state that if the calorie input is less than the energy output, you will lose weight. This is true; HOWEVER, this does not necessarily promote good health.

The gain cycle focuses less on counting calories and more on your mindset and body awareness, encouraging you to make informed choices that promote overall health. The fat loss, improved mood, and increased energy are by-products of the main goal to establish a healthy and sustainable lifestyle.

If you commit to your plan, one day at a time, for 21 days, you will achieve results. After establishing this new routine for 21 days, it will become harder to break the cycle than to continue with it. I particularly like the findings from Philippa Lally, who is a health psychology researcher from the University of London. Her studies found that: "Missing one opportunity to perform the behaviour did not materially affect the habit formation process."

In summary, forming improved habits is not an "all-or-nothing" process. This balance is life. There will never be a "perfect time" to start something because everything is in a constant state of change. Embracing that realisation and adapting your mindset to ensure your

THE GAIN CYCLE

good choices outweigh your bad choices will keep you on track and in the direction of your goals.

NOTES

WHAT DO I NEED?

The only thing you need to know is that you deserve to be happy and healthy, and that every day you make choices that are impacting those two factors in your life. By regretting mistakes of the past, you continue to relive them. Break that cycle now! This program is only one day at a time for 21 days. Time will pass regardless of whether you commit to this program or not, so you may as well see what you can achieve when you follow a quick and easy, highly effective plan!

Seriously, "failing" is not an option. Either way, however closely or loosely you follow this program, you will reach the end of the 21 days. What you do with that and where you end up is entirely up to you.

Thank you so much for trusting me and my program to guide you on the next chapter. This is a truly exciting opportunity that I am grateful to share with you.

Knowing there has to be something better and wanting to make changes, but having no idea where to start. The best place to start is exactly where you are! Right here, right now, THAT is your starting point.

I then assessed what I had been through. I made the hard realisation that each day I think about the hurts and heartaches of my past, I revive them and they continue to plague my present, which negatively impacts my future. In addition to this, I simply reliving this pain was not dealing with it, so it continued to grow, manifesting into this overwhelming wave of sadness, anger and frustration. That cycle had to stop because it was not healthy and in no way beneficial to me, my family, or my goals.

I pulled out my diary and traced a small plate over the page to make a circle. I ruled it into six even sections and labelled each one to cover my process from grief-stricken to empowered. (These are not "six easy steps"; they are confronting, and the more honest you are with yourself, the more effective this process will be)

These sections are:

Reflect:

Reflect on the situation. "Radically accept it" (This is a term my psychologist has frequently used, and it has to do with acknowledging something has happened that you don't agree with; however, you have to accept that it has happened and move on from there, often without an explanation.) There will be people who do not share your belief systems, morals, values, ethics, etc.

Without your acceptance, some people will never change; you prevent yourself from gaining closure to move on. Similarly, you cannot move forward while you are living in and reliving the past.

Resolve

Resolve that you are ready to create change. You have suffered enough, and you deserve to be happy, healthy and strong. You have goals; this is your plan to actively work towards achieving them. USE IT!

Release

Let go of your anger, fear, frustration, anxiety, pain, feelings of sadness or anything else holding you back. This is a very simplistic statement for a very complex matter. You control how you feel, so you need to own those feelings and make a conscious decision to step back (out of the reactive zone). This will allow you to assess and respond to situations in a more rational, less draining manner. This is a challenge, and it will take time to master; however, being aware of this situation is crucial to your success.

Realise

Realise that you can do this. Every choice you make has the potential to improve your situation. Your mindset is instrumental to everything because your perception determines your reality. Follow simple steps daily to improve your mood and shift your mindset from negative to positive gears. How you think will have a physiological effect on your body, which will also influence how you feel.

Refuse

Refuse to accept defeat or feelings of worthlessness, fear or anything that makes you feel overwhelmed. The human body is designed to heal. Your mind is no different; we are all capable of evolving, growing and learning. Be aware of your triggers, stressors and low points, then take action to turn these into strengths. This will take time and lots of substitution and self-reflection.

Repeat.

Repeat. Repeat. Repeat! Consistency and persistence are what create cycles. Commit to yourself and your right to make a sustainable, healthy, and happy lifestyle. This is not to say that every day will be a dream, but it reinforces that one bad day here or there will not undo all of your hard work and good choices to achieve your goals!

Reading these and writing them are completely different processes for you. Please, draw your own circle and write these headings down.

In each sector, I want you to ask yourself and answer the following:

Reflect:

How do I feel now?

What happened?

Why did it happen?

How have I been coping with this?

Why am I motivated to change this cycle?

Resolve:

Am I a victim or a victor?

Are you going to own your own choices? What is your plan for a healthier lifestyle?

What is a goal you will work towards?

What will you achieve in the next 3 weeks?

PLAN:

1. Set a clear bedtime:

2. Set a clear "out of bed" time:

3. Eat consistently, aiming for 5-6 meals:

4. Water goals:

5. Coffee/ tea goals: (limit caffeine)

6. Set a clear exercise goal: 2 x 2-3-minute workouts each day. Am/pm (anything else is a bonus.)

Release:

Write down a positive affirmation for the week: Write down a weekly motivational quote

Why I am doing this: (the more specific your motivation is, the more committed to achieving it you will be)

Realise:

What are my stressors?

What are my coping strategies?

What are healthier alternatives to deal with my stress?

What is working well with my stress management?

I am in control of how I feel and what I think.

I will get outside at least once a day.

I will make an effort to connect with someone each day to say hi.

Refuse:

I will not let a mistake, skipped day, or criticism stop me from committing to this program. I will not sabotage myself. I can follow this plan because I am designing it for myself.

I will not let anyone else or myself make me feel sad.

I will use challenges to set goals and motivate myself to succeed.

THE GAIN CYCLE

Repeat:

All cycles repeat. What I do consistently will determine my success. I will own my choices.

I will strive for improvements

My success is my reward for the work I put in.

I will continue to move closer towards my goals.

Between stages 3 (Release) and 4 (Realise), I identified additional areas for improvement. I needed to visualise my stressors and strategies, and then divide them into categories of distractions and solutions to hold myself accountable and be honest about how I was dealing (or not dealing) with life and the curveballs it was throwing at me.

This allowed me to group my behaviours and focus on more positive solutions. I drew another circle and this time separated it into quarters. I labelled the top sections Stress vs. Address and the bottom sections Distractions vs Solutions. For every stress on the left, I had a strategy to address it.

You need to know and reiterate to yourself: *"I can control my behaviour when I am aware of it and the need to make changes."*

The beauty of this process lies in its simplicity. Confronting and as personal as you choose to make it, but the "work" required to follow this program is minimal, with evident results.

I then took a cup and drew 21 circles in my diary. On the following pages are examples of the circles I use.

On each circle, I have written for you to fill in:

1. Bedtime: _____

2. Wake up: _____

3. AM training: _____

4. Breakfast: _____

5. Snack: _____

6. Lunch: _____

7. Snack: _____

8. Dinner: _____

9. Snack: _____

10. PM training: _____

11. Water / Tea: _____

12. Coffee: _____

Then at the end of each day, I tick what I've done. I wrote the number of estimated litres of water, as well as the number of cups of tea and coffee. Capped to 2 x coffees a day. Aiming for 2-3 litres of water and 5+ cups of peppermint tea.

My training program had to be quick and easy. Something to get me moving, so I thought 10s.

10 x Squats Push-ups

10 x Sit-ups

10 x Bridges

10 x Kneeling kick backs.

That's it. If I want to do more, I will, but that is in addition to this 21-day program. I don't want to continue to up the stakes and feel overwhelmed or stressed; I just wanted to establish something simple and sustainable.

The "magic" is in the simplicity; however, you have to invest the time at the beginning to commit to making changes and have a clear focus on what you want to improve. The Gain Cycle will create change because, as logic dictates, it must.

When you drink more water, get more sleep and fuel your body more consistently with nutrient-rich food, you will feel better. It is almost infuriatingly obvious, yet when I am stressed, busy, or sad, self-care is the first thing I stop to focus on, which then compounds my stress and inability to cope with the challenges at hand.

I want this round of the program to be an opportunity for each of you to tell me what's working, what isn't and offer some one-on-one coaching as well as a group environment for general discussion (adds some variety to my opinions).

The point of this template is that it is entirely customisable so that it can fit in with your abilities, goals, and personal preferences.

I hope that this "Gain Cycle" program makes more sense now that I have explained the process, and you all feel genuinely excited about the improvements that can and will be made by the smallest of changes.

I am so grateful to each and every one of you for allowing me to share this program and my vision with you. The diversity of the group of trailblazers from 2019 is awesome, from health professionals, doctors, fitness professionals, naturopaths, nutritionists, business executives, business owners, writers, hairdressers, real estate administrators, receptionists, swim instructors, artists, super mums, mums to be, photographers, carers, farmers, drafters, tradies, military personnel, police recruits, chefs, surveyors, media crew and producers... I am truly humbled to have such an enriched, open-minded network of skilled and educated people to share this with.

You saying "Yes" to this program without any concrete information or testimonials is a major compliment. THANK YOU for believing in me and being open to trialling this and providing feedback to influence a completely novel way of approaching health and fitness!

NOTES

THE GAIN CYCLE

NOTES

WHERE DO I START?

Bloody great question! This has been a major obstacle for so many. Start at Day One and repeat for Twenty-One days.

THE GAIN CYCLE

Day One

Set a clear bed time:
_____

Set a clear "out of bed" time:
_____

Eat consistently, aiming for 5-6 meals:
_____

Water goals:
_____

Coffee/ tea goals: (limit caffeine)
_____

Set a clear exercise goal:
2 x 2-3 minute work outs each day. Am/pm (anything else is a bonus.)
_____

NOTES

Day Two

Set a clear bed time:
_____

Set a clear "out of bed" time:
_____

Eat consistently, aiming for 5-6 meals:
_____

Water goals:
_____

Coffee/ tea goals: (limit caffeine)
_____

Set a clear exercise goal:
2 x 2-3 minute work outs each day. Am/pm (anything else is a bonus.)
_____

NOTES

THE GAIN CYCLE

Day Three

Set a clear bed time:
_____

Set a clear "out of bed" time:
_____

Eat consistently, aiming for 5-6 meals:
_____

Water goals:
_____

Coffee/ tea goals: (limit caffeine)
_____

Set a clear exercise goal:
2 x 2-3 minute work outs each day. Am/pm (anything else is a bonus.)
_____

NOTES

Day Four

Set a clear bed time:
_____

Set a clear "out of bed" time:
_____

Eat consistently, aiming for 5-6 meals:
_____

Water goals:
_____

Coffee/ tea goals: (limit caffeine)
_____

Set a clear exercise goal:
2 x 2-3 minute work outs each day.
Am/pm (anything else is a bonus.)
_____

NOTES

THE GAIN CYCLE

Day Five

Set a clear bed time:
_____

Set a clear "out of bed" time:
_____

Eat consistently, aiming for 5-6 meals:
_____

Water goals:
_____

Coffee/ tea goals: (limit caffeine)
_____

Set a clear exercise goal:
2 x 2-3 minute work outs each day. Am/pm (anything else is a bonus.)
_____

NOTES

Day Six

Set a clear bed time:
_____

Set a clear "out of bed" time:
_____

Eat consistently, aiming for 5-6 meals:
_____

Water goals:
_____

Coffee/ tea goals: (limit caffeine)
_____

Set a clear exercise goal:
2 x 2-3 minute work outs each day. Am/pm (anything else is a bonus.)
_____

NOTES

Day Seven

Set a clear bed time:
_____

Set a clear "out of bed" time:
_____

Eat consistently, aiming for 5-6 meals:
_____

Water goals:
_____

Coffee/ tea goals: (limit caffeine)
_____

Set a clear exercise goal:
2 x 2-3 minute work outs each day. Am/pm (anything else is a bonus.)
_____

NOTES

Day Eight

Set a clear bed time:
_____

Set a clear "out of bed" time:
_____

Eat consistently, aiming for 5-6 meals:
_____

Water goals:
_____

Coffee/ tea goals: (limit caffeine)
_____

Set a clear exercise goal:
2 x 2-3 minute work outs each day. Am/pm (anything else is a bonus.)
_____

NOTES

Day Nine

Set a clear bed time:
_____

Set a clear "out of bed" time:
_____

Eat consistently, aiming for 5-6 meals:
_____

Water goals:
_____

Coffee/ tea goals: (limit caffeine)
_____

Set a clear exercise goal:
2 x 2-3 minute work outs each day.
Am/pm (anything else is a bonus.)
_____

NOTES

Day Ten

Set a clear bed time:
_____

Set a clear "out of bed" time:
_____

Eat consistently, aiming for 5-6 meals:
_____

Water goals:
_____

Coffee/ tea goals: (limit caffeine)
_____

Set a clear exercise goal:
2 x 2-3 minute work outs each day.
Am/pm (anything else is a bonus.)
_____

NOTES

Day Eleven

Set a clear bed time:
_____

Set a clear "out of bed" time:
_____

Eat consistently, aiming for 5-6 meals:
_____

Water goals:
_____

Coffee/ tea goals: (limit caffeine)
_____

Set a clear exercise goal:
2 x 2-3 minute work outs each day. Am/pm (anything else is a bonus.)
_____

NOTES

Day Twelve

Set a clear bed time:
_____

Set a clear "out of bed" time:
_____

Eat consistently, aiming for 5-6 meals:
_____

Water goals:
_____

Coffee/ tea goals: (limit caffeine)
_____

Set a clear exercise goal:
2 x 2-3 minute work outs each day. Am/pm (anything else is a bonus.)
_____

NOTES

THE GAIN CYCLE

Day Thirteen

Set a clear bed time:
_____

Set a clear "out of bed" time:
_____

Eat consistently, aiming for 5-6 meals:
_____

Water goals:
_____

Coffee/ tea goals: (limit caffeine)
_____

Set a clear exercise goal:
2 x 2-3 minute work outs each day. Am/pm (anything else is a bonus.)
_____

NOTES

WHERE DO I START?

Day Fourteen

Set a clear bed time:
_____

Set a clear "out of bed" time:
_____

Eat consistently, aiming for 5-6 meals:
_____

Water goals:
_____

Coffee/ tea goals: (limit caffeine)
_____

Set a clear exercise goal:
2 x 2-3 minute work outs each day.
Am/pm (anything else is a bonus.)
_____

NOTES

Day Fifteen

Set a clear bed time:
_____

Set a clear "out of bed" time:
_____

Eat consistently, aiming for 5-6 meals:
_____

Water goals:
_____

Coffee/ tea goals: (limit caffeine)
_____

Set a clear exercise goal:
2 x 2-3 minute work outs each day. Am/pm (anything else is a bonus.)
_____

NOTES

Day Sixteen

Set a clear bed time:
_____

Set a clear "out of bed" time:
_____

Eat consistently, aiming for 5-6 meals:
_____

Water goals:
_____

Coffee/ tea goals: (limit caffeine)
_____

Set a clear exercise goal:
2 x 2-3 minute work outs each day. Am/pm (anything else is a bonus.)
_____

NOTES

Day Seventeen

Set a clear bed time:
_____

Set a clear "out of bed" time:
_____

Eat consistently, aiming for 5-6 meals:
_____

Water goals:
_____

Coffee/ tea goals: (limit caffeine)
_____

Set a clear exercise goal:
2 x 2-3 minute work outs each day. Am/pm (anything else is a bonus.)
_____

NOTES

Day Eighteen

Set a clear bed time:
_____

Set a clear "out of bed" time:
_____

Eat consistently, aiming for 5-6 meals:
_____

Water goals:
_____

Coffee/ tea goals: (limit caffeine)
_____

Set a clear exercise goal:
2 x 2-3 minute work outs each day. Am/pm (anything else is a bonus.)
_____

NOTES

Day Nineteen

Set a clear bed time:
_____

Set a clear "out of bed" time:
_____

Eat consistently, aiming for 5-6 meals:
_____

Water goals:
_____

Coffee/ tea goals: (limit caffeine)
_____

Set a clear exercise goal:
2 x 2-3 minute work outs each day. Am/pm (anything else is a bonus.)
_____

NOTES

Day Twenty

Set a clear bed time:
_____

Set a clear "out of bed" time:
_____

Eat consistently, aiming for 5-6 meals:
_____

Water goals:
_____

Coffee/ tea goals: (limit caffeine)
_____

Set a clear exercise goal:
2 x 2-3 minute work outs each day.
Am/pm (anything else is a bonus.)
_____

NOTES

THE GAIN CYCLE

Day Twenty One

Set a clear bed time:
_____

Set a clear "out of bed" time:
_____

Eat consistently, aiming for 5-6 meals:
_____

Water goals:
_____

Coffee/ tea goals: (limit caffeine)
_____

Set a clear exercise goal:
2 x 2-3 minute work outs each day. Am/pm (anything else is a bonus.)
_____

NOTES

ABOUT THE AUTHOR

Tanya Taz Dunstan is an athlete, entrepreneur, business owner of XL Personal Training, health and fitness professional and mother, who designed "The Gain cycle" in 2019 as a lifeline to survive an extremely traumatic event in her life.

"As an athlete who has trained and worked on disciplines to push through any 'low motivation' to achieve my goals, grief hits different, and there was nothing available that I could find to help me go through the motions to just get out of bed and try to function - let alone 'live life." I was at an all time low, drowning in depression with high blood pressure, insomnia, extreme CTSD (Continuous Traumatic Stress

Disorder) and stress disorder due to the shock and trauma of what I was going through and one day laying on my bed I had a very real conversation with myself about whether I was going to make it: "You can't "live" like this - it's literally killing you. No one else is going to save you - if I want to get through this, you have to do it yourself." And so, I systematically designed a step-by-step survival guide to go through the motions of basic self-care for survival to get to a safe space I could then build on with traditional training programs and meal plans for optimal results.

Of all of the programs I have designed, this is the one I am the proudest of because it comes from a place of empathy at the depths of the darkest, most depressed and alone space to help people cope encompassing basic nutrition and exercise principals with mental health foundations for a holistic and well rounded approach for life- not for aesthetic benefits- but to achieve a genuine quality of life. It literally saved my life, and I hope it gives others hope to exercise kindness and just do a little bit each day to stay above water- life doesn't get easier- but with basic self-care principles, like hydration, sleep, sunshine and movement- it is more manageable.

WHATEVER YOU ARE GOING THROUGH - NO MATTER HOW MUCH YOU ARE HURTING, YOU WILL GET THROUGH THIS! IT MIGHT NOT SEEM POSSIBLE RIGHT NOW, BUT YOU WILL EXPERIENCE PEACE, JOY AND HAPPINESS AGAIN.

ABOUT THE AUTHOR

TANYA TAZ DUNSTAN

XL Personal Training/ Health On Tap. Taz Dunstan:
Founder and designer:

https://www.instagram.com/p/B1Z-D0njukQ/

https://www.instagram.com/p/B1aBUnnDT35/

https://www.instagram.com/p/B1aGAn6D6Q9/

https://www.instagram.com/p/B1aJKSRjUH1/

https://www.instagram.com/p/B1vldp9jUgQ/

https://www.instagram.com/p/B1Z_U88DIK3/

THE GAIN CYCLE

"I would never put my name (or face) next to something I didn't trust and respect. (This goes for products I use, people I recommend, and services I provide) I am honoured to be able to provide the first testimonial for "the Gain Cycle", although I know more value will be taken from the testimonials of others who have tried and tested this program.

The trailblazers who test drove the first ever gain cycle have almost completed their 21 days, and when they have... I will share their testimonials to support what this program can achieve and how it has helped each of them."

TESTIMONIALS

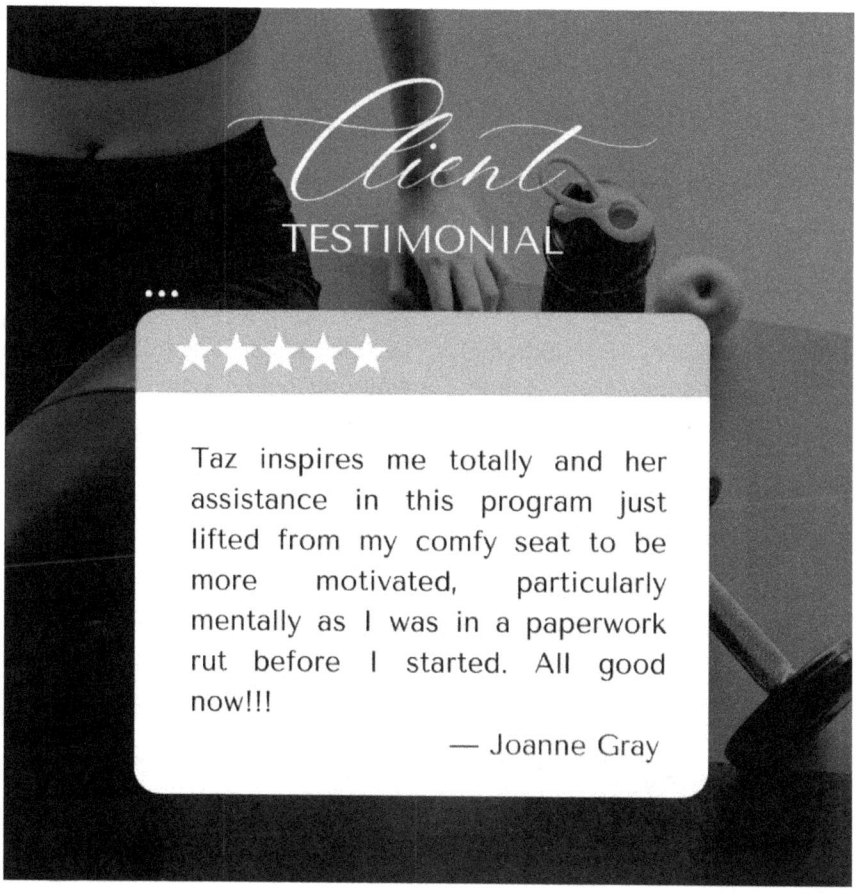

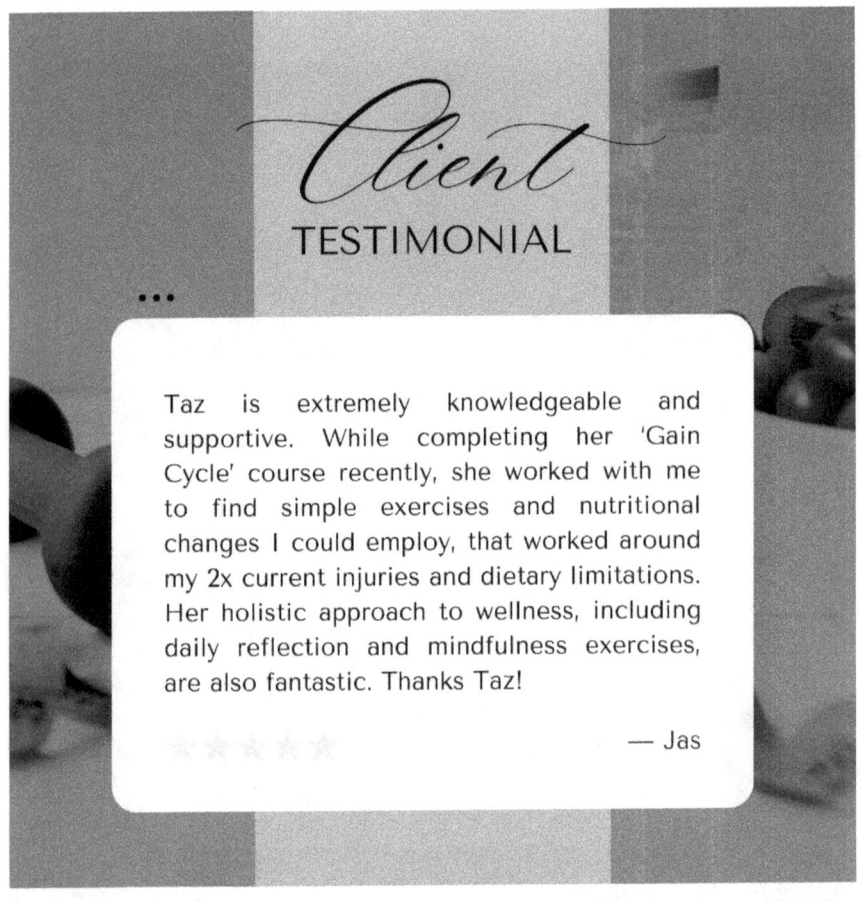

Client TESTIMONIAL

Taz is extremely knowledgeable and supportive. While completing her 'Gain Cycle' course recently, she worked with me to find simple exercises and nutritional changes I could employ, that worked around my 2x current injuries and dietary limitations. Her holistic approach to wellness, including daily reflection and mindfulness exercises, are also fantastic. Thanks Taz!

★★★★★

— Jas

Client TESTIMONIAL

" I learned that it's not too hard to make a start at a healthier life, body and mind. Changing up diet in a tasty affordable way is achievable and improving problem pain areas, lead to being able to handle daily stress and triggering events more positively.

— Rey Biddle

TESTIMONIALS

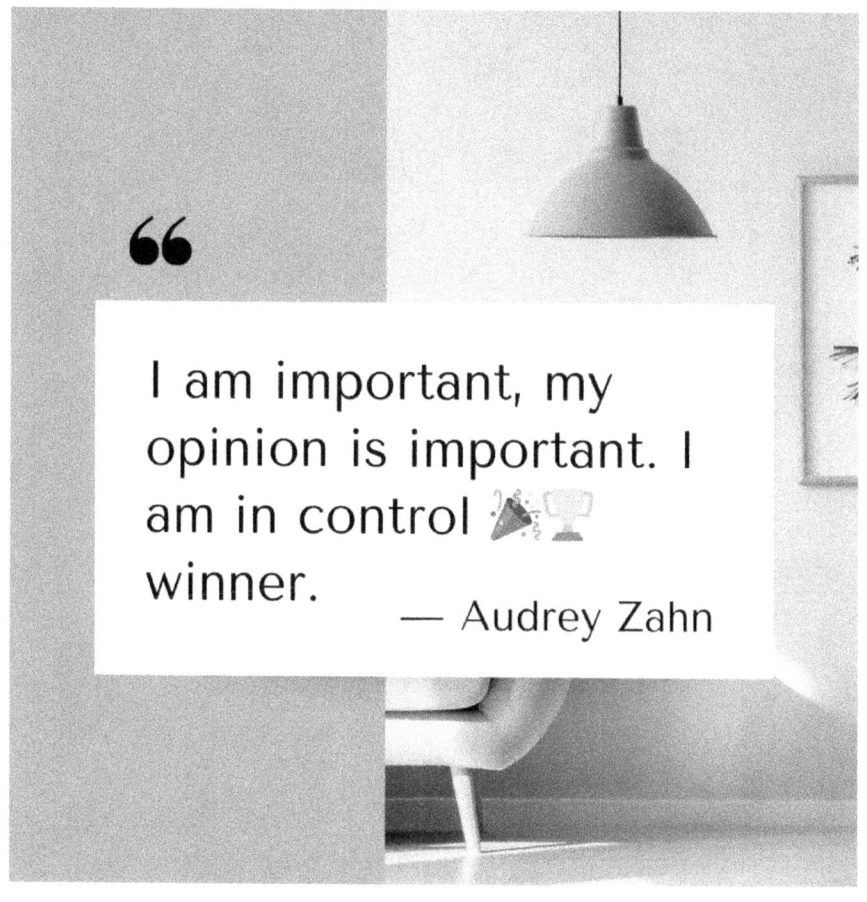

> I am important, my opinion is important. I am in control 🎉🏆 winner.
> — Audrey Zahn

THE GAIN CYCLE

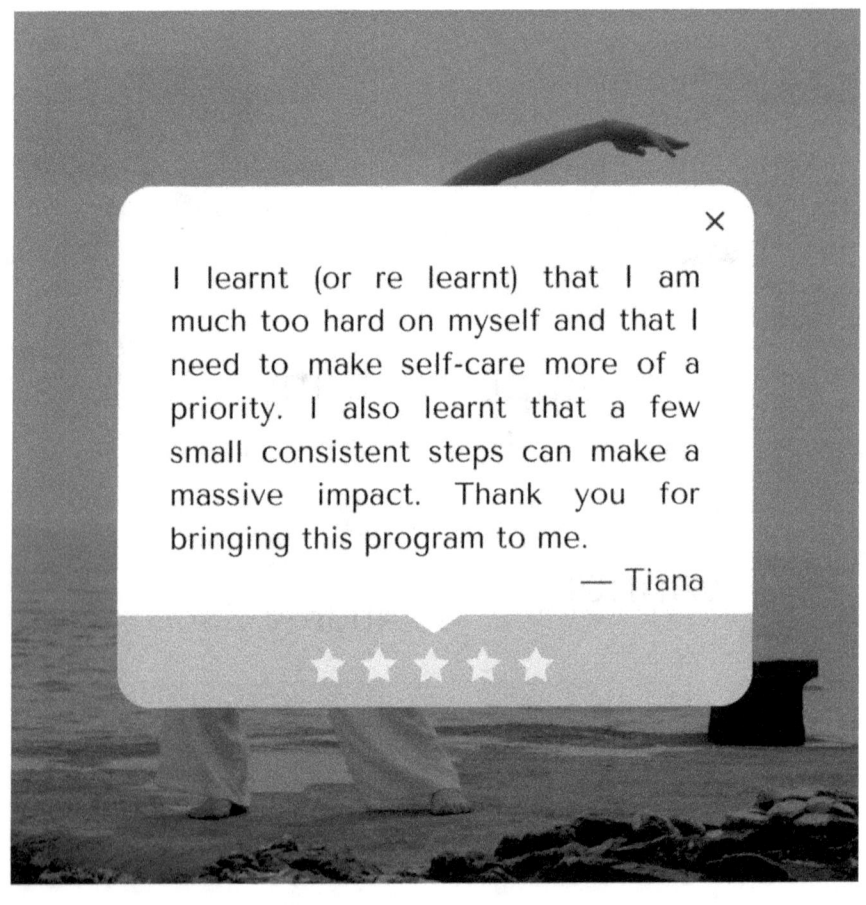

I learnt (or re learnt) that I am much too hard on myself and that I need to make self-care more of a priority. I also learnt that a few small consistent steps can make a massive impact. Thank you for bringing this program to me.

— Tiana

TANYA (TAZ) DUNSTAN CONTACT DETAILS

Websites:

Taz@xlpt.com.au

www.ponsonbychambers.nz

Social Media

Facebook: https://www.facebook.com/Healthontapforthepeople

Instagram:
https://www.instagram.com/taz_dunstan/

www.ingramcontent.com/pod-product-compliance
Lightning Source LLC
Chambersburg PA
CBHW072017060426
42446CB00043B/2639